# The Cathedral of Our Lady in Antwerp

Patrick De Rynck

LUDION

Image sources:
Cathedral of Our Lady, Antwerp, pp. 8, 14, 15, 16 bottom & top, 20 bottom, 24 top, 30 right, 42, 43, 44, 45, 50 and 53.
City of Antwerp, Archaeology Department, p. 5 bottom.
City of Antwerp, Municipal Archive, pp. 6, 17 bottom.
Frank Toussaint, © photography p. 20 top.
Groeninge Museum, Bruges, p. 8 bottom left.
Koninklijk Museum voor Schone Kunsten, Antwerp, pp. 15 top, 36 bottom.
Kunsthistorisches Museum, Vienna, p. 12 bottom.
Musée des Beaux-Arts, Tours, p. 35 right.
Musée du Louvre, Paris, p. 13.
Musées Royaux des Beaux-Arts de Belgique, Brussels, pp. 9, 21.
Museum Plantin-Moretus, Antwerp, pp. 11, 25.
Nono Rongé, © photography p. 49.
Ooidonk Castle, Bachte-Maria-Leerne, p. 10 centre.
Province of Antwerp, Cultural Heritage Department, © photography Bart Cloet and Hugo Maertens, pp. 4, 5 top, 8 top, 10 top, 12 top, 17 top, 18, 19, 22 bottom, 27, 28, 29, 30 upper left, 30 lower left, 31, 32 upper right, 32 lower left, 33, 34, 35 left, 37, 39, 46–47, 48, 49, 51, 52, 54, 58, 68, 76, 77, 78, 79, 80, 81 and 82.
University Library, KU Leuven, p. 7.
Vleeshuis Museum, Antwerp, p. 26.


Translation
Ted Alkins

Editing
Fiona Elliott

Design
Johnny Bekaert. Concept by Griet Van Haute

Layout
Wilfrieda Paessens

Lithography
Die Keure

Printed and bound in China

www.ludion.be
ISBN 90-5544-580-0
D/2005/6328/25

# Preface

## The Cathedral's Tale

The Cathedral of Our Lady in Antwerp is a magnificent and important monument, not to mention the largest Gothic church in the Low Countries. Visitors encountering it ought first and foremost to take away something of the life it has lived so far: its earliest remains; the plans and construction process; how it was paid for; the different roles the cathedral has played; its decoration; the artists who have worked here; the disasters and plundering that have befallen it; and the building's successive refurbishments and restoration.

Its life has resembled that of a person: all the decisions, activities and events that have unfolded here continue to reverberate; and in many cases they have left their visible mark on the cathedral as we find it today. Such a life – and above all that of a building like a cathedral – is also rooted in the biography of its city. In a sense, the cathedral's history is that of Antwerp in microcosm. Hardly surprising then that the city's most famous son, Peter Paul Rubens, should be such a powerful presence here.

This book offers a concise retelling of the cathedral's tale from the early Middle Ages to the present day: a period stretching some nine hundred years. It sets out to answer three questions that might be posed by readers and visitors: what will I see in the cathedral? What won't I see that was once here? And how does everything fit into its historical context?

Patrick De Rynck

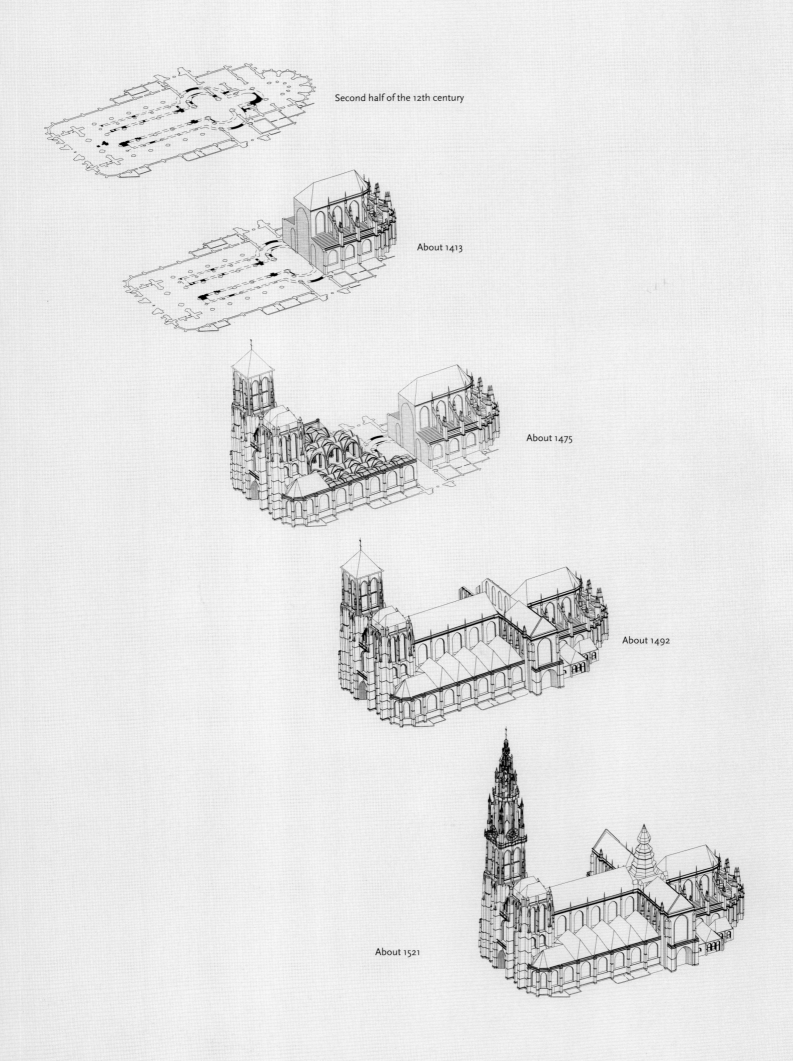

Second half of the 12th century

About 1413

About 1475

About 1492

About 1521

# From Chapel to Cathedral
## The Construction Process

Although work on the Cathedral of Our Lady as we know it today began in 1352, the building's story goes back much further than that. The year in question was undoubtedly a crucial one, but the new edifice was hardly built in a day: the transformation of what was a small chapel into a majestic church would take a good four centuries and cannot be described as complete until around 1520.

Deed of foundation for the Chapter of Our Lady and the church of the same name. It was granted by the Bishop of Cambrai in 1124. The diocese of Antwerp was founded in 1559 and it was only then that the church became a cathedral.

### PRECURSORS

Christian life in Antwerp dates back to the seventh century, when local people first began to be converted. Few if any sources go back that far. The earliest surviving text to refer to the Church of Our Lady was written in 1124 and consists of the deed of foundation of the chapter (the church's administrators). The existing Chapel of Our Lady was elevated to parish church status in that year. It owed its promotion to the fact that Antwerp's existing parish church – St Michael's – had been turned into a Norbertine abbey at more or less the same time. Norbert of Gennep, the Order's founder, was invited to Antwerp in person to attend the event.

Work on a new building commenced shortly after Our Lady's became a parish church – probably in 1132. Prominent churches and their chapters often owned the adjacent land, too. The Church of Our Lady was no exception: in 1220, the Duke of Brabant made it a grant of land, which was quickly used to build a hospital and houses for the canons.

There was a romanesque church on the site of the planned Gothic building when the first stone of Our Lady's was laid in 1352. It was already a big church by the standards of the time, measuring 42 metres across and 80 in length.

### 170 YEARS OF BUILDING

Construction of the largest Gothic church in the Low Countries took almost 170 years – from 1352 to 1518. Work began ten years after the city of Mechelen had started to build the Church of St Rombaut and was largely completed during the Burgundian period. The choir came into use around 1415, while the aisles were finished in 1487. Today's cathedral building with its seven-bay nave stood at the present location by 1518, give or take a few outbuildings. The main reason it took so long to complete was simply the enormous scale of the construction project. But there were political upheavals, too, that flared up just after 1352 and dragged on for several decades. The years in question saw the transfer of Antwerp and Mechelen from the Duchy of Brabant to the County of Flanders. In 1434, meanwhile, the choir was damaged by fire. Finally, the design

Traces of the earliest romanesque building have survived in the shape of fragments of wall in Tournai limestone that were uncovered in the 1980s. They are too few, however, to tell us anything about the church or chapel's appearance.

was modified during the building process: the original plan was for a nave with three bays and a row of chapels on either side; this was subsequently expanded to seven bays, probably because the growing number of altars inside the church was creating problems of space. The changes required the purchase of additional land and the enlargement of the transept – the part of the church running at right angles between the nave and the choir.

### PROUD TOWER

The final part of the church to be completed (around 1520) was the imposing North Tower, which has dominated the Antwerp skyline ever since. Construction of the 123-metre-high tower – which has been described as 'lacework in stone' and a 'filigree masterpiece' – took roughly a hundred years. It is the only Brabant Gothic church tower to be completed; Brussels Town Hall is its secular counterpart. The foundations were laid around 1420 by the master-builder Peeter Appelmans, who, along with his successor Everaet Spoorwater, worked on a front with two towers until 1475, when construction of the South Tower was halted. It remains in that unfinished state today, with three levels and a height of 65 metres. A fourth level was added to the North Tower around 1480, but further construction then also stopped, as attention shifted for the next quarter of a century to other parts of the church.

Work on the North Tower resumed in 1502, with a new design by master-builder Herman de Waghemakere or his son Dominicus. The fifth stage was completed five years later, with the pinnacle added shortly before 1520. This was too late for the South Tower to be finished, as plans for a new and much larger church had already been drawn up. The lower parts of the North Tower are quite plain and so it is to its final stages that the structure owes its reputation as 'lacework in stone': the pierced stonework of the windows is much more pronounced and the carved decoration is more abundant, while the area around the clock seems entirely open. The structure is narrower at the top, with flying buttresses linking the

Anonymous, *Imaginary townscape with the second romanesque church* (complete and detail), *c.* 1200, watercolour, 26 x 373 cm. Illustration in L. van Caukercken, *Chronyke der stadt Antwerpen*, 1688–1693, fol. 136bis. The accompanying text reads: 'The dean and canons began to work on the Chapel of Our Lady of the Branch to enlarge it. They built a choir there.'

¶ In laudem insignis opidi Antwerpien versus.
Candida que peperit concordia menia patrum
Neptuni cursu sors redimire studet
Discat posteritas mores seruare parentum
Succrescant partis vt potiora bonis
Amplificet vires sic munera rector olympi
Augeat:et euo sic rogat antwerpia
Subdita que pollet florens sub tegmine sacri
Cesaris:hec suadet iussa tenere senum.

Anonymous, *Antwerp Harbour*, c. 1515, printed by Jan de Gheet. Coloured woodcut, 20,5 x 17,2 cm. View of Antwerp harbour with the unfinished West Front of the Church of Our Lady. The square section of the North Tower's pinnacle is roughly half complete.

## The cathedral: Brabant Gothic

The Gothic church – the largest in the Low Countries – was completed around 1520. It is an example of the style known as 'Brabant Gothic', characterized by the play of space, light and verticality. The nave of the cathedral has seven bays. The middle aisle has only two storeys. The clustered columns have no capitals and reach up into the cross-ribbed vaulting. Together with the pointed Gothic arches, this gives the nave its lofty and slender impression. The choir too is high and full of light, while the aisle around it has five ambulatory chapels. The choir itself is linked to the nave by the transept. The cathedral's floor plan is that of a cross basilica.

Jan Provoost, *Donor with St Nicholas* (wing of a triptych), *c.* 1514, oil on wood, 120.5 x 78.5 cm. View of Antwerp harbour before the North Tower was completed.

Some early studies of the architectural history of the cathedral claimed that the West Front had two completed towers. This engraving is based on another by Wenzel Hollar in 1649.

The North Tower

four little corner turrets to the main body of the tower. It was here that the Renaissance made its entrance: after a century of construction, the cathedral tower achieved a sense of unity through its very diversity. According to several local legends, the devil himself was left green with envy by the architectural quality of the North Tower.

## THE MASTER-BUILDERS

The cathedral was a prestigious project on which several celebrated master-builders were employed. Most of them were active in more than one place in a region that boasted prosperous towns like Brussels, Leuven, Diest, Tienen, Aarschot, Mechelen, Antwerp, Breda, Bergen-op-Zoom, Middelburg and Dordrecht. Their area of activity more or less coincided with the old Duchy of Brabant, hence the description 'Brabant Gothic'. The term is actually rather misleading, as substantial differences exist between the architecture labelled in this way.

- Jacob van Thienen might have designed the choir, although some historians believe it was the work of another, anonymous master-builder. Van Thienen also worked in Brussels on the Town Hall and Church of St Gudule.
- Everaet Spoorwater (also called Everaet van Veeweyden; up to 1474) worked primarily in the southern part of what is now Holland; he continued the construction of the towers and nave.
- Herman de Waghemakere (1430–1503) and Matheus Keldermans the Younger began the final stage of construction of the nave, the transept and the crossing. They also designed the pinnacle of the tower.
- Dominicus de Waghemakere (1460–1542) and Rombout Keldermans the Younger (c. 1460–1531) completed the pinnacle, which put the finishing touch to the cathedral. They were also commissioned to design a new and much bigger choir, marking the beginning of what was to be a considerably larger church. ■

## A twelfth-century heretic

*St Norbert Preaching against Tanchelm's Heresy*, seventeenth century, oil on wood, 68.5 x 88.6 cm, Brussels, Musées Royaux des Beaux-Arts de Belgique. Seventeenth-century interpretation of a controversial episode in history. The completed cathedral is shown in the background.

Could it be that we owe the cathedral to a heretic? The penitential preacher Tanchelm was active in Antwerp around 1110. If contemporary reports are to be believed – and we have to be extremely careful, as they were invariably produced by his enemies – he and his followers encouraged worshippers to turn against the Church and key elements of its teachings, including the doctrine of Transubstantiation. He is alleged to have 'married' the Virgin Mary and to have molested women. Others stated that Tanchelm railed against the abuses of certain priests. He ordered his followers to boycott church services and to withhold their ecclesiastical taxes or 'tithes'.

Tanchelm was murdered by a priest in 1115. His actions and those of his followers supposedly led to Norbert being invited to Antwerp to restore order, and hence to the reorganization of local ecclesiastical structures and the creation of the Parish of Our Lady. The story of Norbert and Tanchelm is, however, one in which truth and legend are closely interwoven, and so we ought to treat it with great caution.

## Church or cathedral?

Throughout most of its history, Our Lady's was 'just' a church, rather than a cathedral. A cathedral is the principal church of a diocese and the permanent location of the bishop's seat (*cathedra*: hence 'cathedral'). It also has to be in the city in which the bishop is officially installed. Its uses include the ordination by the bishop of new members of the priesthood. The diocese of Antwerp was not created until 1559, several decades after the church that was to be its cathedral was completed. Prior to that date, Antwerp belonged to the bishopric of Cambrai, now in northern France. It was also in 1559, therefore, that the Church of Our Lady was elevated to cathedral status. The diocese was abolished in 1801, during the French occupation, and was not restored until 1961.

Incidentally, the word *dom* is sometimes used in the Netherlands and Germany to describe a cathedral; like the Italian *duomo*, it comes from the Latin *domus* or 'house'.

# Four Catastrophes and Two Centuries of Peace

## 1533–1800

The sixteenth century was Antwerp's Golden Age: the city became a centre of international trade, its economy boomed and its population doubled in the space of a few decades, reaching around 55,000 in 1526 and as many as 100,000 in 1565. Having boasted no more than 10,000 inhabitants in 1350 – the period in which the building of the cathedral began – the port on the river Scheldt was now a metropolis of European stature. The income of the church fabric – the building's administrators, who managed its assets – grew in proportion to the wealth of the city. In the latter part of the sixteenth century, however, Antwerp was hit by several years of intense religious and political strife. The fate of the cathedral was to mirror that of its city.

Frans Francken the Elder (1542–1616), *Jesus among the Doctors* (central panel), 1587. This is the central panel of one of the few sixteenth-century altarpieces that remain in the cathedral as triptychs. Commissioned by the Guild of Schoolmasters and the Guild of Soap-Boilers, who shared a chapel, it tells the Gospel story of the 12-year-old Jesus who slipped away from his parents to debate with the 'doctors' or scribes in the Temple, shown here with a Renaissance interior. Mary and Joseph have just arrived.

Anonymous, *The Fire at Antwerp Cathedral*, seventeenth century, oil on wood, 45 x 36 cm. Impression of the fire of 1533.

### 1533: DEVASTATION BY FIRE

On 15 July 1521, just as the cathedral's construction was coming to an end, Emperor Charles V laid the foundation stone of what was to be a new and much larger choir. The ceremony was intended to mark the beginning of a megalomaniac expansion of what was already a sizeable church. The new project would have been one of Europe's most prestigious undertakings ever, resulting in a church with a floor plan no less than three times what it is now, surrounded by five towers.

The hugely ambitious plans never came to fruition, not least because of what happened on the night of 5 to 6 October 1533, when a badly snuffed candle set fire to an altar by the North Tower. The blaze spread to the wooden rafters of the middle aisle and the transept, the vault of which had yet to be completed. Considerable damage was inflicted on the building itself and its fittings. The new project was shelved and all the available funds were redirected in the years that followed to restoring the battered cathedral.

### 1566: ICONOCLASM

The 'Iconoclastic Fury' descended on Antwerp and its cathedral on 19 August 1566, the day the image of the Virgin Mary was carried in procession to celebrate the Feast of the Assumption. It had broken out a week earlier in the small town of Steenvoorde on the modern Franco-Belgian border. Protestant reformers – especially the Calvinists – viewed the worship of images as idolatrous: no such decoration was tolerated in their own, sober churches. Catholics, by contrast, failed to see the problem, provided that the image was being venerated as a representation of God, Christ or one of the saints and not in its own right. The reaction hit Antwerp and its cathedral like a hurricane: brief but devastating. Dozens of works of art were destroyed in what were in all likelihood carefully planned attacks. The municipal authorities responded

Vergilius Bononiensis, *Map of Antwerp* (detail), 1565. A whole series of small houses were built against the cathedral choir in 1565, rents from which provided the church fabric with additional income. There was to be a recurring debate in subsequent years between those who believed the cathedral ought to be 'freed up' (the *degagisten* as they were dubbed) and those who preferred things as they were (the *antidegagisten*).

quickly, ordering the local craft guilds on 9 September to clear up the rubble and to rebuild their smashed altars and the altarpieces that went with them.

### 1578–85: CALVINIST RIGOUR

The wave of image-smashing reflected a deeper-seated division in the society of the Low Countries. One side remained loyal to the Church and to Spain, while the other was made up of Protestant reformers and people opposed to Spanish rule. The prolonged conflict between the two groups was eventually dubbed the Eighty Years' War (1568-1648). The repercussions for Antwerp included a period of Calvinist rule from 1578 to 1585. In November 1576, poorly paid, mutinous Spanish troops went on a murderous rampage through the city that came to be known as the 'Spanish Fury'. The cathedral emerged unscathed, only to be faced in the early 1580s with the prohibition of Catholic worship and the renewed

Gaspar Bouttats, *The Iconoclastic Fury of 1566 in the Cathedral*, second half seventeenth century, etching, 25.9 x 38.1 cm. The Spanish caption reads: 'The violence and sacrilege with which the heretics attacked images of Christ and the saints in Antwerp Cathedral.' The 1566 architecture and interior are not depicted accurately.

Peter Neefs the Elder and Bonaventura Peeters the Elder, *Interior of the Cathedral*, oil on wood, 50 x 70 cm. This small panel shows the ceremonial reception of Archduke Wilhelm Leopold by the clergy in 1648. It also provides a useful glimpse of the cathedral's appearance in the aftermath of the Eighty Years' War.

stripping away of Catholic fittings and art from its interior.

The tide turned again in 1585, when the Spanish general Alexander Farnese recaptured Antwerp and re-established Catholic worship. As had occurred two decades earlier, the guilds were instructed to reinstall their altars. Yet the results of the conflict for Antwerp were dramatic: the young Dutch Republic closed the river Scheldt, trade restrictions were imposed and the population halved, leaving only 45,000 residents in 1586. Many fled to the Protestant North: artists, merchants and scholars among them. Although Antwerp bounced back to a remarkable extent in the decades that followed, it did not fully recover until the nineteenth century.

### TWO 'QUIET' CENTURIES

Having come through the turbulent sixteenth century, the cathedral was spared any fresh assaults for over 200 years. The Southern Netherlands remained Catholic and subject to Spanish rule. The region's governors, Archduke Albert and the Infanta Isabella, issued a decree in 1611 ordering the restoration of churches damaged during the religious troubles, money for which was collected during Mass. The Low Countries had just embarked on the armistice known as the Twelve Years' Truce (1609–21).

The seventeenth century was a period of refurbishment for the cathedral, and for the acquisition of numerous new works of art. The eighteenth was a time of peace and stabilization, and was also marked by the rise of important new movements within society: the emergence of rationalism, with its scientific and technical discoveries, the Enlightenment and increasing secularization, and the gradual bringing under state control of areas like relief for the poor and education, which had hitherto been the preserve of the Church. The Spanish

Netherlands passed into Austrian hands, with rulers like Charles VI, Maria Theresa and Joseph II, who were not afraid to intervene in ecclesiastical affairs. Yet it was from France that the next hurricane was to strike.

### THE 1790S: TABULA RASA

The events of the 1790s were to define the cathedral's interior as we see it today: the French Revolution was accompanied by a desire to wipe out the old ways. The first danger signs became apparent in November 1792, when the French marched into Antwerp. The reaction was a mixture of disquiet and relief at the longed-for liberation from the Austrians. Remnants of the *ancien régime* came under threat, most notably the nobility and the Church, along with their visible symbols and trappings. The French ordered that inventories be drawn up of all the Church's property.

1794 was a disastrous year for the cathedral: the Bishop of Antwerp quit his residence forever on 21 July, while shortly afterwards, the occupying forces demanded payment of a gigantic sum of money by the city. The Church's contribution consisted of gold and silverwork – chalices, ciboria and monstrances – much of which was simply melted down.

That same summer, many of the paintings in the cathedral were removed in the name of the *Représentant du Peuple*; the order was carried out by a lieutenant who was himself a portrait painter. The French were especially interested in work by Peter Paul Rubens, but they also confiscated paintings by Otto van Veen, Frans Floris and Wenzel Coeberger. The works were shipped to Paris, where they were received with great ceremony. Back in Antwerp, the coats of arms of the Knights of the Golden Fleece that had hung in the cathedral choir

Benjamin Zix, *The Imperial Retinue Visiting the Musée du Louvre after the Wedding of Napoleon Bonaparte and Archduchess Marie-Louise on 2 April 1810* (detail), watercolour, 24 x 172 cm. The group is depicted as it passes Rubens's *Descent from the Cross*.

Drawing of the Cathedral by Jan Blom

were publicly burned as symbols of the hated *ancien régime*.

The Austrian Netherlands were officially annexed by France in 1795. Priests who did not want their churches to be shut down were obliged to swear an oath of loyalty to the Republic, to which another was added a few years later declaring 'hatred of the kingdom'. All the same, most churches were closed, while abbeys, confraternities and guilds were abolished and their goods confiscated. These – assuming they had not already been plundered – were then publicly auctioned: buildings, land, furniture, floors, art treasures and all. As the new century dawned, the cathedral was a desolate sight: deserted and full of rubble.

### JAN BLOM: THE EVASIVE SAVIOUR

The French Revolution saw the interior of the cathedral stripped bare and the building itself endangered. The response to these twin threats included acts of civil disobedience: to save some of the building's contents, Antwerp citizens occupied 'their' cathedral and removed a number of items. Meanwhile, they refused – or did not dare – to bid for any of the lots offered for auction. The upshot of this, however, was that many important works of art were sold for bargain prices to outsiders. When a Brussels man tried to have the high altar and several tombs loaded for shipping, local dockworkers refused to cooperate until threatened with violence.

One or two priests took the hated oath to the Republic in the hope of being permitted to reopen their churches, thereby shielding them from further harm. Permission for the cathedral to reopen, however, was refused and it was proposed that the building be turned into a museum. A committee was given the task of determining which 'scientific and artistic artefacts' were to be retained for the École Central du Département des Deux-Nèthes – the French version of the city's academy.

There was one extreme threat from which there would have been no coming back: demolition. Some people had their eye on the building materials, while others wanted to create more

Barend van Orley (1491/92–1542), *The Last Judgement and the Seven Acts of Mercy*, 1519, oil on wood, 248 x 218 cm and 248 x 94 cm (x 2). One of the two triptychs to survive the fire of 1533.

space for a new 'Place de l'Égalité'. Municipal Architect Jan Blom was ordered to measure up the church to prepare for its demolition. Blom played for time, offering a series of excuses as to why he could not complete the job, including an injured thumb, which prevented him from drawing, and the unhealthy conditions in the church. His delaying tactics were to save the cathedral: following Napoleon's seizure of power, the new Consulate adopted a much softer line than its predecessor, the Directoire. The reopening of confiscated church buildings was not permitted as yet, but at least the cathedral would now survive, albeit picked clean. ■

## Lost art

Adriaan Lommelin, High Altar, seventeenth century, engraving, approx. 47 x 33 cm.

Most of the works of art produced for or installed in the cathedral have been destroyed, have disappeared without trace or are now kept at another location. Here are some striking examples of lost gems:

– 1533: all but two of the altarpieces perish in the fire. Losses include the carved wooden retables for which Antwerp's craftsmen were so renowned. The two surviving works were triptychs that can now be seen at the Koninklijk Museum voor Schone Kunsten in Antwerp: Quentin Massys's *Lamentation over the Dead Christ* (1508) and Barend van Orley's *Last Judgement* (1519).

– 1566 and 1581–85: the fury of the iconoclasts was directed primarily at religious sculptures, but organs, altars and retables were also damaged or destroyed.

– French period: the cathedral was stripped bare in the 1790s and the Baroque high altar was destroyed. It might have been designed by Rubens, who was also responsible for the painting above the altar (*The Assumption of the Virgin*), which *did* survive and which was returned in 1815. The lost pieces were replaced by early-nineteenth-century works, some of which incorporate earlier elements.

# Towards Today's Cathedral
## The Nineteenth and Twentieth Centuries

Most of the rubble had been removed from the cathedral by April 1800 and the refurbishment of the almost empty church could begin: the work was to take more than a century to complete. But how should the interior of the 300-year-old, plundered Gothic church be restored? Not to mention the fact that the structure of the building itself was also in urgent need of repair. Yet all was not doom and gloom: Antwerp was able to celebrate in 1815 when works by its prodigal son, Rubens, were returned from Paris.

Artus Quellinus the Younger (1625–1700), *St Anthony of Padua with the Christ Child*, late seventeenth century, polychrome wood, height 160 cm. The abbey church of the Antwerp Franciscans was shut down during the French period and later turned into a museum and academy of fine arts. The statue of St Anthony was moved to the cathedral.

Paul Lauters, *View of the Interior*, c. 1830, coloured lithograph, 29.8 x 21.4 cm. The church had been partially redecorated by 1830. The Gothic Revival, which began to take shape around 1840, was, however, still some way off.

### THE EARLY YEARS OF RESTORATION

The large organ over the ambulatory and a single altar belonging to the Young Crossbowmen's Guild remained in the cathedral in 1800. Other items – including marble columns and stairs, pillars and pilasters from the rood screen and tomb decorations – were still present only because their buyers had failed to collect them. Some were repurchased, while others were given back by the people who had bought them at auction. Fourteen works of art also quickly found their way home. These had been earmarked for the École Central – the new academy the French were planning to create. Seventeen other altarpieces were not returned but were placed, through the Academy, in what is now the Koninklijk Museum voor Schone Kunsten in Antwerp. Their previous owners – craft guilds – had been abolished and were not to be reinstated.

## WORK FROM ELSEWHERE

The cathedral collection was to reap a sad harvest in the early nineteenth century, when it became home to a series of artistic orphans: works that had belonged to other churches or abbeys prior to the French Revolution, but which had been left homeless by the destruction of their original location or its cooption for an entirely different purpose. Here are some of the main examples:

- The cathedral was restored using the floor from the church at the Abbey of St Michael, which, on Napoleon's orders, had been partly demolished and turned into a shipyard;
- The same church provided two fine statues of Saints Peter and Paul (c. 1630) by Rubens's contemporary and friend Hans van Mildert;
- The figure of St Anthony from the Venerable Altar came from the Franciscan monastery, which had been turned into an academy;
- Michiel Van der Voort's unique pulpit (1713) was purchased from the demolished church at the Abbey of St Bernard in Hemiksem near

Willem Jacob Herreyns (1743–1827), *Supper at Emmaus*, 1808, oil on canvas, 310 x 240 cm. As work began in the early nineteenth century to restore the all-but-destroyed and empty cathedral interior, a neo-classical style was initially adopted. The 1840s, however, saw the advent of the Gothic Revival. Rubens's influence on painting was still apparent around 1800, as in this canvas by Herreyns, which the painter presented to the Venerable Confraternity for its chapel. The painting shows the moment at which the disciples recognize Christ at the inn of the small village of Emmaus: their risen Lord breaks the bread and gazes up towards heaven.

The return to Antwerp of paintings by Peter Paul Rubens that had been carried off to Paris, 1816

Antwerp, together with six confessionals and a Communion bench.

## RUBENS IS BACK!

In the aftermath of the Battle of Waterloo in 1815, a representative of King Willem I of the Netherlands, to which the future country of Belgium now belonged, travelled to Paris with a committee from Antwerp. Their mission was to locate the works of art that the French had removed from the cathedral and other churches and to bring them home again. The committee did its work well: by the time it left Paris on 31 October, it had taken possession of most of the relevant works. On 5 December, the paintings were given a ceremonial reception to mark their return to Antwerp. All the

François Durlet (1816–1867), Choir stalls (detail), 1840–83, oak. Prior to the French period, choir stalls were used during the regular prayers of the cathedral chapter, which consisted of the canons attached to the church. Since the chapter was abolished in 1797 and not reinstated until 1965, these stalls – which some consider to be the cathedral's most important neo-Gothic feature – date from a time when there were no canons here. The lavishly decorated scenes in high-relief for each of the 36 seats depict episodes from the life of the Virgin Mary. They also feature coats of arms, saints, angels and symbols. Most of the carvings are now safely in storage.

same, works that were no longer in Paris but had been moved to other French cities (including Lille, Tours, Nancy and Nantes) were never recovered. As far as the cathedral is concerned, that meant the loss of four paintings, among them *Alexandre Goubau and His Wife Anne Anthony with the Virgin Mary* by Rubens, and works by De Vos and Coeberger. Rubens's painting is still in Tours to this day, due to the misidentification of the sitters as Christophe Plantin and his wife. Plantin was born in Tours, which was seen as sufficient reason not to return the painting.

### NEW OR OLD STYLE?

The focus throughout the nineteenth century was on the interior of the cathedral. There was one major difference compared to the time before the French Revolution: neither the craft guilds nor their altars were reinstated, although old confraternities like the Guild of Our Lady of Praise and the Venerable were granted new altars. New monumental tombs were also installed, partly on the initiative of the Moretuses – a prominent local family.

The restoration of the cathedral initially occurred in the late-eighteenth-century late-Baroque and neo-Classical styles; there were also calls, however, for the work to be done in a style more in keeping with the original architecture, which was Gothic. The Gothic style became associated in certain circles – not without a touch of nostalgia – with a society that was still thoroughly religious.

Little heed was paid at first to champions of the Gothic Revival; in 1839, however, choir stalls in that style were installed in the cathedral. The architect was the 23-year-old François Durlet, who was put in charge of the overall restoration process in 1844. In the decades that followed, he consistently opted for the neo-Gothic style that he made his own, unleashing a revivalist wave upon the church: leading woodcarvers worked on the new choir stalls until 1883; polychrome, carved Gothic retables were installed on the altars of many of the chapels; work also began in the 1830s on elements of the church building itself, including the towers, transept and choir. The restorers gave the cathedral a more Gothic appearance than it had ever had before.

It is for that reason that today's building has so much neo-Gothic painting, furniture, stained-glass windows, statues and architecture. The five ambulatory chapels in particular were thoroughly refurbished in the neo-Gothic style, down to the flooring and silverwork. Views on the Gothic Revival were and remain mixed: some consider it to be little more than imitation, while others believe that neo-Gothic restoration gave the cathedral a renewed sense of unity and harmony.

## RESTORATION: MOVEMENTS IN A PERPETUALLY UNFINISHED SYMPHONY

Following the restoration and modifications of the nineteenth century, it was not until the 1960s and the re-establishment of the diocese of Antwerp in 1961 that a new round of restoration work was embarked upon. Earlier plans fell foul of a series of crises, most notably the two World Wars, although the Church of Our Lady was thankfully spared any new calamities during those two global conflicts. Such was the scale of the necessary restoration work, which continues to this day, it was split into several stages:

- The first of these was devoted to restoring and fire-proofing the roof (1969-72).
- The nave was then restored (interior refurbishment: 1973–83), together with the South Tower and the West Front (exterior refurbishment). Modern lighting was installed, plus a sound system and climate control. The repairs carried out during this stage included the stone facing of columns disfigured as far back as the fire of 1533: the response in the sixteenth century had been simply to plaster over the damage.
- A transitional stage then followed in the 1980s, in which archaeologists and art

Jean-Baptiste van Wint (1827–1906; carving) and Jean-Baptiste Anthony (1854–1930; paintings), *The Seven Acts of Mercy*, 1897–98, oak and oil on wood. This neo-Gothic triptych 'in the medieval style' was hailed by the press in 1898 as 'masterly, full of character and harmonious'. It is a combination of carving (central element) and painting (wings). The central part is devoted to the life of St Vincentius a Paulo, while the wings deal with other saints.

historians were able to refine their knowledge of the building and its history, to help them make the right choices in subsequent stages. It was confirmed, for instance, that the interior had been brightly painted from its very earliest days. All the same, it was decided not to restore the paintwork fully, as the shift in style would have been too abrupt. In the end, the painting was confined instead to the ambulatory chapels.

- Attention shifted in 1990–93 to the transept and choir. The restored cathedral was ceremonially re-inaugurated on 2 April 1993.
- Work then began in 1994 on restoring the ambulatory and its neo-Gothic chapels, followed by the exterior refurbishment of the nave and choir and the ongoing restoration of the interior. ▪

The nave of the cathedral during the restoration in the 1970s

## Nello and Patrasche

Bronze statuette of Nello and Patrasche in Kapelstraat, Hoboken

The Franco-British writer Marie-Louise de la Ramée (Ouida) visited the Church of Our Lady in Antwerp in 1871, like many thousands before and after her. The trip inspired her to write a romantic tearjerker called *A Dog of Flanders*, which was subsequently turned into several films. In it Ouida describes the life of a poor boy called Nello and his dog Patrasche. Nello would love to be a painter like Rubens, but his poverty leaves him with very few opportunities. He enters a drawing competition, the first prize in which is a bursary to study at the academy, only to find the results are fixed in favour of a richer boy. Throughout his young life, little Nello tries to catch a glimpse of Rubens's beautiful paintings in the cathedral: something that was not so easy at the time, as the triptych was covered with a curtain and only revealed in return for payment. Nello, of course, did not have any money. After a series of adventures, Nello and Patrasche find themselves at the cathedral one Christmas Eve. Nello slips into the church after Midnight Mass and in the moonlight is finally able to view the marvellous triptych, which had been opened to mark the occasion. He then dies of exhaustion in front of *The Descent from the Cross*. The story is a set text in Japanese primary schools, prompting many Japanese tourists to follow in Nello's footsteps to view Rubens's *Descent*.

# More Than a Place of Worship
## The Cathedral and Its Many Functions

Churches in the Middle Ages – and for many years after that – were lively public spaces in which society came together. People expressed their faith and celebrated key moments in their lives there, as they continue to do to this day.

### LIFE IN THE CHURCH

If we walked into the cathedral in 1600 we might see a priest celebrating Mass at one of the many altars and another doing the same in a chapel in which members of a confraternity have assembled. Yet another altar is being used for a baptism or a wedding ceremony. The canons in the choir are singing their canticles as people wait to make their confessions. A procession makes its way out of the cathedral, carrying the Sacraments to anoint the sick. A gravedigger is opening up the floor, while a beggar by a column hopes for alms from his wealthier fellow townspeople. Nobles and small groups of prominent individuals gather to discuss the news of the day. Joiners and a lone painter get on with their work as the barking of dogs echoes around the cathedral. A young mother leads a sulky child by the hand as they take a shortcut through the church.

Things are much quieter and calmer these days, although the cathedral remains a place of worship where Christians come to express their unity with one another and with God. Ecumenical services are held, too, in which a similar sense of togetherness can be shown towards other religions. Masses are graced by music, most notably that of the organ, and by the voices of the cathedral choir and the Girls' Chorus. They also take place, of course, among the same outstanding works of art that draw

Peter Neefs the Elder, *Interior of the Cathedral*, oil on wood, 59 x 84 cm

Anonymous, *Sacramental Procession Leaving the Cathedral*, *c.* 1700, miniature, 41.5 x 29 cm,
illustration from the 'Golden Book' of the Confraternity of the XIV-Day Anointment. People
suffering from prolonged illnesses were visited once a fortnight to bring them the Holy Sacrament.
The confraternity was created to add prestige to the custom.

thousands of tourists every year from all over the world. The time-honoured Venerable Confraternity and Guild of Our Lady of Praise still hold their processions to the high altar on important feast-days, and after all these centuries, the cathedral is still dedicated to the Virgin Mary.

## HOUSE OF TWO SAINTS

Two holy figures have been of central significance to the cathedral, ever since its foundation as a parish church: the Virgin Mary, for whom it is named, and to a lesser extent St Norbert. Mary, whom many Catholics view as the most important intermediary between humanity and God, is also the patron saint of Antwerp itself. The Guild of Our Lady of Praise was founded in 1479 to celebrate evensong every day. The guild had its own chapel, complete with organ and singers. The statue of the Virgin is kept in that chapel to this day, and the guild itself is still active, too. The current figure dates from the sixteenth century and replaces an earlier one that was destroyed during the period of Calvinist rule. Mary is everywhere in the cathedral: painted or carved in marble, stone or wood, in a variety of styles and from different periods.

As described in the first chapter, St Norbert is linked to the year in which the parish church was founded (1124). He is said to have restored respect for the Eucharist by successfully combating the heretic Tanchelm and his followers. Meanwhile, an important brotherhood at the cathedral – the Venerable Confraternity or Confraternity of the Holy Sacrament – has been devoted to the Eucharist for centuries and remains so to this day. Already in existence by 1446, its members were local citizens who set up their own chapel, altar and services at the church.

Anonymous, *Interior of the Cathedral*, c. 1630 (?), oil on wood, 71 x 105 cm, unknown collection

Marten Pepijn (1575–1643), *St Norbert*, 1637, oil on wood, 158 x 120 cm. St Norbert, dressed in the habit of the order he founded, is shown kneeling before the Holy Sacrament. The Sacraments were a central focus of the Catholic Counter-Reformation, which helps explain the popularity of saints like Norbert, who enjoyed a special association with the Eucharist. The artist Marten Pepijn was a contemporary of Rubens. The panel has been in the cathedral only since 1823, having previously hung in the Abbey of St Michael.

Our Lady of Antwerp, sixteenth century, polychrome wood, height 180 cm. This miraculous figure is still the object of devotion, especially around the Feast of the Assumption on 15 August. Like many similar cult objects, the rather solemn image of the Virgin Mary and the Christ Child has several sets of robes.

Guillielmus Kerrickx (1652–1719), *Two Reliefs with Attributes of the Coopers' Guild*, 1683, white marble, *c*. 67 x 101 cm. These reliefs were part of the marble altar enclosure of the coopers' guild. They were carved by Guillielmus Kerrickx, who incorporated symbols of the profession like barrels, tools, bunches of grapes and vine-leaves.

Hendrik van Steenwijck the Elder, *Interior of the Cathedral of Our Lady*, 1583 or 1593, oil on wood, 45.2 x 62.5 cm, Budapest, Szépmüvézeti Museum

## ALTARS

One of the main differences between churches today and how they were before the French Revolution is the number of altars and the paintings and sculptures that went with them. The Cathedral of Our Lady, for instance, had dozens of altars in the seventeenth century: around fourteen confraternities had their own, as did about six militia companies and twenty or so craft guilds, each representing a particular occupation (such as the bakers, millers, furriers, brewers, stocking makers, linen weavers, rag dealers, painters and fishmongers).

Confraternities began to spring up at a very early date; they founded chantries to support the priests who performed the religious services at their altars. Wealthy citizens also founded chantries and dedicated Masses, for their own souls' salvation and to promote worship in general. Between 1232 and 1547, for instance, there were 116 foundations of this kind: little wonder that building plans in that period had to be revised from time to time.

Some of the altars located in aisle or ambulatory chapels could develop into mini-churches, with their own sacristy and a separate entrance. The majority, however, were installed against a column in the nave. They were often used by several different groups, especially when the cathedral was going through its latest bout of construction or rebuilding. Owners vied with one another to have the biggest, richest and most beautiful altar. Marble or wood enclosures were built around them, which only the priest was allowed to enter. Most of the altars are no

Anonymous, *The Church of Our Lady*, 1568, woodcut, 24.8 x 34 cm. This illustration from Lodovico Guicciardini's celebrated travel book *La description de tout le Païs Bas* shows how small houses were built against the nave and the choir to raise money for the church fabric.

Anonymous, *The Church of Our Lady and the Cemetery*, 1597, oil on wood, 47 x 65 cm. Burial inside the church was a privilege reserved for well-to-do parishioners.

longer present and all the enclosures have disappeared. But some of the works of art that were originally associated with them and which managed to survive the cathedral's various upheavals are now distributed around the building, the best-known example being Rubens's *Descent from the Cross*.

### WHO PAID FOR IT ALL?

Who financed the building and maintenance of the Cathedral of Our Lady? Put simply, the church fabric was responsible for commissioning construction work and alterations. Its most important figures were the treasurer (a canon) and the churchwardens, who were often town councillors. Accounts were submitted every year to both the chapter and the city council.

The Church of Our Lady was only a parish church until 1559, but for many years it was the only one in Antwerp. It had to raise its income from the parish itself, the chapter and the city. What did that mean in practice? Worshippers were obliged to receive the Sacraments – Baptism, Confirmation, Eucharist, Marriage, Confession, Ordination and Extreme Unction – in their own parish and to pay for the privilege. That made funerals, weddings and baptisms a particularly important source of income. Meanwhile, the city had its own chapel in the cathedral and was responsible for one of the towers, which also served as a lookout post from which to warn citizens of fire or attack. Both were paid for by local tax-payers. On top of this came bequests from deceased parishioners, indulgences and penitential offerings, donations for worship (of miraculous statues, for instance), income from the annual fair and from a covered market on church land at which painters, woodcarvers and book dealers could sell their wares, rents for the small shops built against the church and other returns from the chapter's land holdings. The set-up as a whole must have been somewhat reminiscent of an estate agent's business.

The construction or enlargement of other churches (St James's, St Andrew's and St Walburga's) introduced a new element of competition for Our Lady's in the early sixteenth century when it came to the allocation of church funds. New parishes meant a redistribution of income, just as the reformer Martin Luther was railing against the sale of indulgences, from which the Church had been earning a considerable amount of money.

Jacob de Backer (c. 1555/1560–1585/1590), *Last Judgement*, with wings added later showing Christophe Plantin with his son and his patron saint, Christopher, and his wife Jeanne Rivière with her daughters and her patron saint, John. The celebrated Antwerp printer and publisher Christophe Plantin commissioned this painting as a commemorative work to be placed over his tomb. De Backer was much in demand for compositions of this kind. The Last Judgement is a perfect theme for a memorial painting, while the inclusion of the donor, his wife and their children in the wings, accompanied by their respective patron saints, is also typical. A little red cross over a child's head meant that he or she had already died.

Burials inside churches – a privilege reserved for the wealthiest parishioners – were permitted until the end of the eighteenth century. Only the most prominent citizens could expect to be buried in the choir. Important figures like bishops and other dignitaries could commission monumental tombs for themselves, accompanied by sculptures or paintings with appropriate themes.

The original idea behind this tradition was that the presence of the mortal remains (or some of them) of a saint or martyr would protect the building, which is why they were to be found in so many churches. Over the centuries, the number of graves in the Cathedral of Our Lady grew into the thousands: at times, up to eight coffins were stacked on top of one another.

The city authorities put pressure on the Church to bury people in the cemetery but, judging from the numerous ordinances they felt obliged to issue, interment inside the church proved stubbornly persistent. Joseph ii banned the practice in 1784 as understanding of public hygiene finally tipped the balance against it.

# A House Full of Art
## The Cathedral and Its Art Works

The interior of the cathedral has something in common with the night sky: just as the constellations we see are formed by the light of stars that actually existed in separate ages, the inside of the church is at once the product of different eras and a coherent entity of its own. To continue the analogy, many of the stars that once lit up the firmament are no longer visible, just as a great deal of the art produced for the cathedral over the centuries has since disappeared, having been destroyed, stolen, sold off or moved. Conversely, much of what we now see would not have been here if earlier works had not needed to be replaced. It is no coincidence that artistic commissions tended to be concentrated in the years following the successive disasters to befall the building: the fire of 1533, the Iconoclastic Fury and the Calvinist period (1566 and 1581–85), and the French Revolution (1794–1800).

### PAINTED WALLS AND CEILINGS

People today often think that the walls, columns and vaults of church interiors were always white – 'the colour of purity' – and that wooden statues were their natural brown hue. Nothing could be further from the truth. Large expanses of the interior were intensively decorated in the Middle Ages, with both figurative scenes and painted motifs intended to accentuate the architecture. Sculptures, meanwhile, were multicoloured or 'polychrome'. Medieval people disliked bare materials, hence this powerful urge to paint. Corporations, guilds and confraternities often had emblems and coats of arms painted near their altars in the church.

'Primitive' (i.e. medieval) art was looked down on in later periods, leading ultimately to the whitewashing over of murals and ceiling paintings: something that occurred primarily in the seventeenth and eighteenth centuries. In the nineteenth century, some of the more enthusiastic Gothic Revivalists proposed repainting the cathedral 'like it used to be' – something that had already been done else-

Anonymous, *Calvary with St Sebastian*. This mural dates from before 1476. Its unusual double theme – the crucified Christ *and* the martyrdom of St Sebastian – reflects the fact that the chapel was used by two groups until 1476: the Confraternity of the Sacred Cross and the Old Crossbowmen's Guild, which had Sebastian as its patron saint. The coats of arms belong to the Bode family: a perpetual Mass was instituted in 1398 in memory of Jan Bode, who was murdered. The mural was rediscovered and repainted in the nineteenth century.

< Example of a vault painting from the South Aisle that was uncovered during the recent restoration. It dates from 1475, before the construction of the cathedral was complete. The enigmatic design features stars, the sun, the moon, and the names of Jesus, Mary, Catharine and John.

where in Flanders. The intense debate that followed eventually led to a compromise: the ambulatory chapels would be repainted, but the rest of the church would be left white. Several old paintings were uncovered during the recent restorations, just as happened in the late eighteenth century.

### COLOURFUL AND ELOQUENT WINDOWS

Only the most prominent citizens or venerable institutions like abbeys or the city council were able to present the church with stained-glass windows, in which the individuals responsible were keen to have themselves included. The earliest documented donations of this kind to the cathedral include one by the knight Willem van Berchem in 1391 and another paid for in 1408 by three citizens of Antwerp who were ordered to do so as punishment. Only two windows – now heavily restored – survive from before the great fire of 1533. They were made in 1503, around the time the cathedral was finished. The fragile glass was frequently among the first victims of any new disaster. The cathedral now has 55 stained-glass windows from different periods of its history.

The early seventeenth century – the height of the Counter-Reformation – was one of the most intensive periods in terms of glass production. Archduke Albert and the Infanta

Isabella paid for a window incorporating their portraits in the transept, as did King Philip III. Sadly, the latter did not survive.

New windows were also installed during the refurbishment of the stripped cathedral in the nineteenth century. A whole series was subsequently added in the 1870s and 1880s, primarily in the aisles and the ambulatory chapels and mostly featuring historical themes connected with the Christian faith in Antwerp. The local firm of August Stalins and Alfons Janssens was responsible for much of the work.

### FURNITURE WITH A STORY

The most noteworthy elements of the cathedral's furniture include the pulpit, Communion benches and confessionals, all three of which

Grotesques comprising foliage and vines, musician angels and birds, 1593, wall painting. This Renaissance mural was uncovered in 1989–90. It stands out oddly now in the Chapel of St Joseph, which is otherwise decorated in the neo-Gothic style. The paintings were done after the death of Canon Gaspar van den Cruyce (1555–1593), who founded a chapel here dedicated to St Ursula.

Ludovicus Willemsen (1630–1702), Communion bench, oak, 1680. This Communion bench was made for the Chapel of Our Lady of Praise but can now be seen in the Chapel of St Anthony. It is made up of seven panels, each with one or two beautifully executed angels holding Marian symbols: a star, a sun, a garland of roses, a censer and a lily stem.

The Adoration of the Magi, c. 1537. Many new stained-glass windows were installed in the aftermath of the fire of 1533. This one was donated by Burgomaster Jacob Dassa and his wife Barbara Rockox: the donors are shown kneeling at the bottom. God looks down from the upper right to witness His newborn Son's reception in the world, as represented by the shepherds and the three 'kings'.

are closely related to the seventeenth- and eighteenth-century Counter-Reformation. During that period, the Church placed special emphasis on the Sacraments, which had come in for particular criticism by Protestant reformers. Confession and the Eucharist are two of seven Sacraments, whereas Protestants recognize only Baptism and the Lord's Supper. Preaching was initially targeted against Protestant doctrines as part of a major counter-offensive. Lavish and imposing pulpits helped bolster the fire-and-brimstone sermons delivered from them.

Communion benches were a new development in the seventeenth century: churchgoers had previously been expected to take Communion at least at Easter (i.e. once a year). From the beginning of the seventeenth century, by contrast, they were instructed to partake of Christ's body on a monthly basis – a requirement that created new needs.

Since worshippers had to be free of sin before they received the consecrated Host, the sacrament of Confession also increased in importance. Although this had existed since the fourteenth century, the confessional itself is another piece of furniture that originated in the Counter-Reformation. It was introduced by the Council of Trent (1545–63), which shaped the Catholic Church's principal reactions to the Reformation.

### A CHURCH FILLED WITH MUSIC

Whenever the cathedral came under attack, the organs were invariably amongst the worst hit: especially in 1566 and the 1790s. A single seventeenth-century organ-case has survived *in situ*, above the West Entrance. It was made in Antwerp in the 1650s by the woodcarver Erasmus Quellinus the Younger, the sculptor Peter Verbrugghen the Elder and the joiner Michiel Boursoy, although it has been altered several times since. Like much of the cathedral's contents, it was sold in 1798 but was never removed, so that the church's administrators were able to buy it back in 1804. A new Metzler organ was installed above the southern ambulatory in 1993 – a rare contemporary feature in the cathedral interior.

Our Lady's can look back over an exceptionally rich musical tradition, including celebrated organists like John Bull, Hendrik Liberti (in the 1650s) and many others. The organists were also responsible for training the choristers: singers brought in to bolster the choir of canons in return for board, lodging and education. Their presence is recorded as early as 1362. Johannes Ockeghem, who would become composer and choirmaster to the king of France, was a chorister here in 1443–44.

### WEALTH OF STATUES

In addition to being a centre of painting, Antwerp was home to many talented wood and stone carvers in the seventeenth century and the cathedral was decorated with a considerable amount of new sculpture in that period: interior and exterior doorways, figures of the Apostles against the columns of the nave and grand monumental tombs for former bishops of Antwerp. Much of the work in question was destroyed during the French Revolution, although some of it has survived, including two monuments to Bishop Capello, who died in 1676. The tomb itself is by Artus Quellinus the Younger, who belonged to a celebrated family of sculptors. Hendrik Frans Verbrugghen – another member of a local sculptors' dynasty – made a second memorial to Capello. As the seventeenth century progressed, sculpture gradually overtook painting in importance.

Artus Quellinus the Elder? (1609–1686) or Peter Verbrugghen the Elder? (1615–1668), *Pieta*, polychrome wood, height approx. 147 cm, second half seventeenth century. A wooden figure of Our Lady of the Seven Sorrows made by Peter Verbrugghen the Elder in 1657–58 was an object of devotion in the cathedral. The statue stood in the ambulatory, lit by lamps and dressed in a variety of different robes. According to nineteenth-century sources, this sculpture is by Artus Quellinus the Elder. It disappeared from the church during the French Revolution, but was given back around 1848.

# The Master
## Peter Paul Rubens in the Cathedral

It seems paradoxical that Antwerp painting should have reached its zenith with the trinity of Peter Paul Rubens, Anthony van Dyck and Jacob Jordaens *after* the sixteenth-century 'Golden Age' and the huge capital and brain drain that the city suffered at the end of that century. The explanation can be summed up in one word: 'Counter-Reformation'. Churches and abbeys had to be restored after the Iconoclastic Fury (1566) and the period of Calvinist rule, but now with even greater splendour, militancy and clarity of message than before. It was against this aggressively Catholic backdrop that Antwerp's greatest artist, Peter Paul Rubens (1577–1640), received numerous commissions, including five paintings for the cathedral. Three of them can still be seen in the church today – or rather they can be seen here again. And they have been joined by another work – the magnificent *Raising of the Cross*.

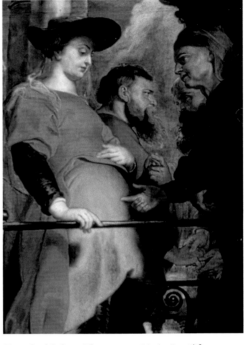

Peter Paul Rubens *The pregnant Maria*. Detail from *The Descent from the Cross* (1611–1614), see p. 59.

Cornelis Cussers, maker, and Jan Baptist van der Veken, designer, *Archduke Albert and the Infanta Isabella Worshipping the Cross*, 1616. The governors of the Southern Netherlands – Elizabeth of Hungary and Albert the Great – kneel in prayer before the crucified Christ, accompanied by their patron saints. Albert and Isabella contributed substantially to Antwerp's burgeoning prosperity in the early seventeenth century thanks to the period of peace that accompanied their rule.

**CONTEXT: COUNTER-REFORMATION**

The Church, supported by the region's governors, Albert and Isabella, strengthened its grip on society in the early-seventeenth-century Southern Netherlands, following the previous decades of strife and competition with the Calvinists. A period of religious militancy now dawned, in which members of the nobility and other prominent individuals were active; they had much to gain, after all, from maintaining the status quo. Religious orders were supported and places of pilgrimage and worship promoted. The sacrament of the Eucharist and veneration of the Virgin were both given a new prominence, while publishers and printers were subjected to scrutiny and censorship.

Churches that had been destroyed or plundered were rebuilt or refurbished; not in the former Gothic style, however, but the new Baroque. Doctrines that the Protestants rejected were actively highlighted, while the abuses within the Church that had helped spark the reformist rebellion in the first place were finally tackled. Under Spanish rule, Church and State formed a seamless unity. The Jesuits were among the most vigorous champions of the Counter-Reformation; their zeal was focused on achieving a single goal: to place the Catholic Church's influence firmly on the traditional pillars of classical Antiquity and early Christianity. Art, architecture, literature, education and everyday life were all permeated in the Southern Netherlands at the beginning of the seventeenth century – the period in which Rubens came to prominence – with the pugnacious Catholicism of which the Jesuits were the standard-bearers. This was the Church from which Rubens received many of his commissions.

## The master's master

Rubens was employed in Otto van Veen's workshop from 1594, the year he turned seventeen, until 1600. Having started out as an apprentice, he became a free master in 1598. The Leiden-born Van Veen was a celebrated artist in Antwerp and he also carried out commissions for the cathedral, three of which can still be seen there today: *The Last Supper, The Raising of Lazarus* and *The Raising of the Widow's Son of Nain*. It was Van Veen who urged Rubens to visit Italy, as he had done himself: the younger artist took his master's advice and spent the period 1600–08 in the South.

Otto van Veen (1556–1629), *The Last Supper*, 1592, oil on canvas, 350 x 247 cm. This masterpiece by Van Veen served as the altarpiece in the Venerable Chapel or Chapel of the Holy Sacrament, which was devoted to the Eucharist. That explains the choice of subject, which the artist has set in a Classical-style hall with columns, oil lamps and a large jug of wine. We see the moment at which Jesus blesses the bread and the wine, thereby instituting the sacrament of the Eucharist. The red-haired Apostle who turns away to have his cup filled is the traitor Judas.

Peter Paul Rubens, *The Resurrection of Christ*,
1611–12, oil on wood, 138 x 98 cm and 136 x 40 cm

## ART AND ITS RULES: THE BAROQUE

The style associated with the Counter Reformation is known as 'Baroque'. Much of Baroque art set out to proclaim the message of the 'One Truth' of Catholic faith. It did so noisily and with considerable grandeur, theatricality and drama, seeking above all to play on the emotions. All this is evident in the intense play of colour, lavish decoration and emotionality of so many sculptures and paintings from that period.

At the same time, new rules were being formulated for religious art. Around the middle of the sixteenth century, the Council of Trent set out the requirements that artists had to meet when handling Catholic imagery. Their art had, for instance, to be readily understood by ordinary people: lesser details were to be omitted; and religious themes had to be dealt with in an elevated (i.e. not everyday) manner. God was no longer to be shown in human form and nudity was to be avoided, other than as a means of eliciting sympathy or connoting poverty and desperation. Popular legends and traditions were to be treated with caution. That was the theory, anyway: things often turned out differently in practice.

Peter Paul Rubens, *The Virgin and Child Worshipped by Alexander Goubau and his Wife Anne Anthony*, c. 1615–20, oil on wood, 124 x 84 cm. This memorial painting consists of a single panel but, as in a triptych, the donors are shown worshipping Mary and Jesus 'in perpetuity'. There is more information about this painting in chapter 3: 'Towards Today's Cathedral'.

Closed shutters with two angels

Detail 'Nicolaas Rockox'

Peter Paul Rubens (1577–1640), *Christ in the Straw*, *c*. 1618, oil on wood, 138 x 98 cm. Rubens painted this work as a memorial for the tomb of Jan Michielsen (†1617) and Maria Maes (†1633). Their patron saints are shown in the wings: Mary (left) and St John the Evangelist (right). The panel was confiscated from the cathedral in 1794 and later presented to the city's museum in 1815.

### 1611: FIRST CATHEDRAL COMMISSION

By 1611, the 34-year-old Rubens had been back from Italy for several years and had become an established artist. Although he had been appointed court painter to Albert and Isabella, he was still allowed to run his expanding studio in Antwerp. Philanthropist, humanist, art-lover and burgomaster Nicolaas Rockox (1560–1640) was involved with a commission to Rubens for Antwerp's Town Hall; he subsequently ordered a second large painting from the artist – a triptych devoted to *The Descent from the Cross*. The painting was destined for the altar in the Chapel of the Arquebusiers' Guild in the cathedral's South Transept. Rubens described Rockox, who was the dean or headman of the guild, as his 'friend and patron'. The guild's patron saint was Christo-

pher, who appears in one of the two wings. The triptych is still in the cathedral: no longer in the chapel for which it was painted, but in the South Transept.

### 1611–12: MEMORIAL ART

Rubens painted the triptych of *The Resurrection of Christ* (p. 34) for the tomb of Jan Moretus – Christophe Plantin's son-in-law – and his widow Martina Plantin around the same time as *The Descent from the Cross*. The commission came from Martina. The theme of the central panel is an appropriate one for a memorial: the triumphant Christ rises up from his rocky tomb to the amazement of the soldiers standing guard. The husband and wife's respective patron saints are shown in the wings: John the Baptist on the left and St Martina on the right.

Peter Paul Rubens
(1577–1640),
*Assumption of the
Virgin*, 1625–26,
oil on wood,
490 x 325 cm

### TWO MORE MEMORIAL PAINTINGS

Three of the five paintings that Rubens produced for the cathedral were intended for the tombs of prominent Antwerp figures. Only *The Assumption of the Virgin* is still in the church: *Christ in the Straw* can now be seen at Antwerp's Koninklijk Museum voor Schone Kunsten, while the third work, *The Virgin and Child Worshipped by Alexandre Goubau and his Wife Anne Anthony*, belongs to the Musée des Beaux-Arts in Tours.

Donating a work of art to a church was equated in the Counter-Reformation with making an offering to God. The donor hoped to elicit the mediation of saints, to ensure his or her place in the Heavenly Jerusalem. Artists had a whole series of requirements to satisfy: there were the Church's instructions regarding the depiction of particular themes, the patron will have had his or her own wishes and the pictorial language had to be comprehensible to worshippers, who were supposed to pray for the donor's soul.

### 1625–26: A NEW PINNACLE

The Virgin Mary became a pivotal figure in the Counter-Reformation, partly due to the Protestants' minimization of her role as intermediary between humanity and God, as a result of which she was much loved in the Middle Ages. The Counter-Reformation saw Catholicism as victorious over Protestantism: a triumphalism represented not least by the figure of Mary.

Towards the end of 1611, the canons of the cathedral chapter commissioned Rubens to paint an *Assumption of the Virgin* for the new marble high altar. The story of Mary being borne bodily aloft to heaven does not appear in the Bible: it arose instead during the Middle Ages, as a result of which Protestants rejected it. That rejection led in turn to its exceptional popularity in the Counter-Reformation. Some theologians also had grave reservations about 'legends' of this kind and it was not until 1950 that Pope Pius XII declared the Assumption an article of Catholic belief. The story tells how the Apostles, who had spread out in every direction to proclaim the faith, were miracu-lously returned to the Holy Land as Mary's death approached. They were present at both the moment of the Virgin's death and three days later when she rose from the grave and was carried up to heaven by angels.

Rubens's first version was rejected, probably because the work was too small; it later found its way into the Church of St Charles Borromeo, also in Antwerp. He did not start on a second until 1625. It was to be paid for by Dean Johannes del Rio, who would be given a grave in the ambulatory in return. The lengthy gap between the two assignments is a sign of Rubens's busy schedule as a painter, the manager of a successful studio and, increasingly, a diplomat. He worked on the second version in the church itself, and it was during this period that his first wife, Isabella Brant, died in 1626. Rubens has included her in the painting, presumably as a tribute: she is the woman in the eye-catching red gown bending over the empty tomb. Isabella's death was one of the rare moments at which Rubens the Stoic offered a glimpse of his emotions, writing of her that: 'She was all goodness and honour. These qualities made her beloved of all, and all mourned her death. It is a great loss that fills me with intense emotion. The only remedy for all troubles is Forgetfulness – Time's daughter. It is her assistance I must now seek. It will be difficult to put sorrow from my mind.'

Detail 'Isabella Brant'

### 1815: A NEW RUBENS FOR THE CATHEDRAL

Rubens did not paint *The Raising of the Cross* for the cathedral, but for the Church of St Walburga, which was closed and demolished in the French period. It used to hang there above the high altar. Along with many other paintings originally done for churches, it ended up in the museum at Antwerp. In 1815, however, an exchange was agreed: because *The Raising of the Cross* formed such a fine pair with *The Descent from the Cross*, the work was given to the Church of Our Lady. In return, the museum received Frans Floris's *Fall of the Rebel Angels* and Rubens's *Christ in the Straw*.

Viewers were shocked by the realism that Rubens brought to bear in this highly religious scene: yet it is precisely the element of flesh and blood within this otherwise utterly spiritual theme that lends it its power. The physicality of Rubens's Christs, Marys and saints makes them real people. This unique work is a fine example of the two traditions that permeated the artist's life and work: the classical and the Christian. Far from seeing any contradiction between the two, he managed to fuse them perfectly in his work. As Rubens expert Kristin Lohse Belkin has put it, 'Rubens' Christ is truly God made flesh'.

Many other painters worked for the cathedral in Rubens's time, among them Hendrik van Balen, Deodaat Delmonte, Frans Francken the Younger and Cornelis de Vos. A younger contemporary called Cornelis Schut provided another outstanding work for the crossing tower: his 1647 *Assumption of the Virgin*. Situated 43 metres above the ground, it shows Mary being carried up to heaven: the perfect theme for the lofty crossing dome. Schut spent a considerable amount of time in Italy, with its tradition of painting Baroque vaults and domes. Work like this required artists who were highly skilled in visual effects that verged on illusionism and in perspective and foreshortening. In this instance, Mary, who has almost reached the highest heaven, is surrounded by a writhing mass of angels. Viewed from the outside, the structure of the 56-metre-high crossing tower takes the form of an onion. It is best viewed approaching the cathedral from Groenplaats. ■

Cornelis Schut (1597–1655), *Assumption of the Virgin,*
1647, oil on canvas, diameter 580 cm

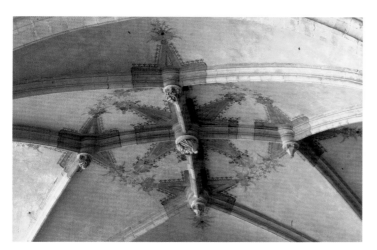

Ambulatory chapels

The crossing – the point in the church
where the nave, transept and choir meet – is
octagonal in structure. The dome is decorated
with carved pendants in the shape of foliage,
including vines, bunches of grapes and oak
leaves. They date from 1497–98 and are located
at a height of 30 metres. The tondo painting
was done in 1647.

The Altar of Our Lady was rebuilt in 1825 by Jacob Jan van der Neer the Younger (1760–1838). It includes seventeenth-century components such as the reliefs with scenes from the Life of the Virgin by Artus Quellinus the Younger (1625–1700) and the globe, which was made by Peter Verbrugghen the Elder (1615–1686) or by Quellinus again.

One of the reliefs shows the meeting between Mary and her cousin Elizabeth. Their respective husbands, Joseph and Zechariah, shake hands to one side, while an angelic figure leads the donkey away.

Jean-Baptiste Bethune (1821–1894),
*The Exaltation of God by the Arts*, 1872

This imposing neo-Gothic stained-glass window was designed by one of the leading lights of the Gothic Revival. It comprises eight lancet windows, each with three registers and devoted to a specific 'art'. A shield-bearing angel at the bottom holds a banderole stating the name of the relevant discipline: navigation, metalwork, architecture, painting, law and rhetoric, poetry and philosophy, theology, and music. The next register up features a figure from the Bible, with the patron saint of each art at the top. The fifth lancet from the left – the one devoted to law and rhetoric – includes the coat of arms of Antwerp, reflecting the fact that the city fathers were primarily lawyers.

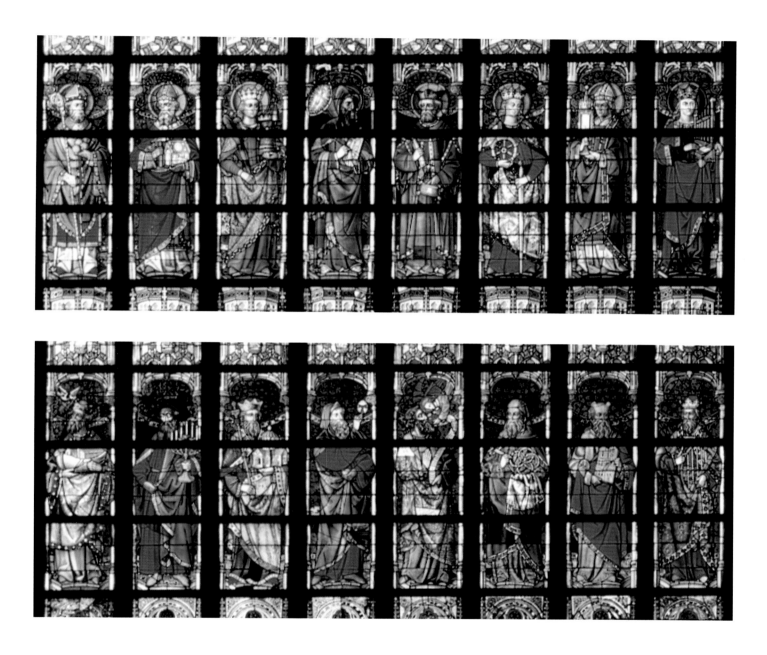

Robert van Olim (1506–1551),
*The Conversion of St Paul*, 1537

The interior refurbishment of the Church
of Our Lady began almost immediately
after the great fire of 1533. This stained-
glass window was a gift of the Fuggers,
the celebrated family of bankers. Anton
Fugger – financier to Emperor Charles –
is shown praying in the bottom left,
accompanied by his patron saint, Anthony.
The window can still be seen in its original
position in the middle aisle.
It tells the story of the conversion of
St Paul, who, having been thrown from his
horse, sees a vision in the sky of Christ
giving his blessing. Jesus's words can be
read on the banderole: *Saule, Saule, quid
me persequeris?* (Saul, Saul, why do you
persecute me?). The window was restored
in 1877 by the Stalins & Janssens company,
which also made new stained-glass
windows for the cathedral.

*Johannes del Rio praying
before the cross, 1615*

Marten de Vos (1532–1603), *The Marriage at Cana*,
1596–97, oil on wood, 268 x 235 cm

The theme of Christ's first miracle was
a natural choice for the Tavern-Keepers'
Guild when it came to refurbishing the
cathedral in the wake of the Calvinist
period. When the wine ran out at a
wedding party, Jesus sent for water and
turned it into a fresh supply of wine.

Mary, the chief steward and Christ pointing

It was a custom in the Low Countries to hang three crowns over the head of the bride and the guests on either side of her, as we see here. Despite the Venetian influence, Marten de Vos continued to work in the Flemish tradition, too, which included close attention to detail.

Peter Paul Rubens (1577–1640), *The Descent from the Cross*, 1611–14, oil on wood, 421 x 311 and 421 x 153 cm (x2)

The three panels of Rubens's triptych depict individual scenes. The wings focus on the beginning of Christ's life and the central panel on its end:

In the middle, a group of people is lowering Christ's body from the cross to wrap Him in the shroud: they are Joseph of Arimathea, Nicodemus, St John and two assistants, together with the Virgin Mary, Mary Magdalene and another woman;

In the scene on the left, the pregnant Mary meets her cousin Elizabeth, who is also pregnant with John the Baptist (the theme is known as the 'Visitation'). They are accompanied by their husbands, Joseph and Zechariah. The servant-woman with the basket of travel items indicates that Mary and Joseph are coming to stay;

The right-hand panel shows the presentation of the Infant Christ to the High Priest Simeon in the Temple at Jerusalem. The kneeling Joseph holds the traditional offering of two doves.

### The backs of the wings

When the triptych's shutters were closed, viewers saw an image of St Christopher carrying the Christ Child while a hermit shines his light. The giant figure of the saint was inspired by an Antique image of the mythological hero and strongman Hercules, which Rubens had seen in Italy. According to a medieval legend, Christopher once carried the infant Jesus across a river. The child was extremely heavy as he was burdened with all the sins of the world. Christopher was the patron saint of the arquebusiers; however, following doubts as to his historical authenticity, the Council of Trent sought to stamp out his cult in the sixteenth century, making his inclusion in an altarpiece problematical. Rubens solved the dilemma by moving the saint to the less prestigious closed shutters.

Despite his marginal position, it is Christopher who provides the key to the altarpiece: his Greek name 'Christoforos' means 'Christ-bearer' and although the different scenes do not narrate a single story, the leitmotif is indeed 'the carrying' of Christ. He is carried in the open triptych in his mother's womb on the left and by Simeon on the right; in the central panel, meanwhile, his body is held up by a group of people, including St John (the figure with the red cloak).

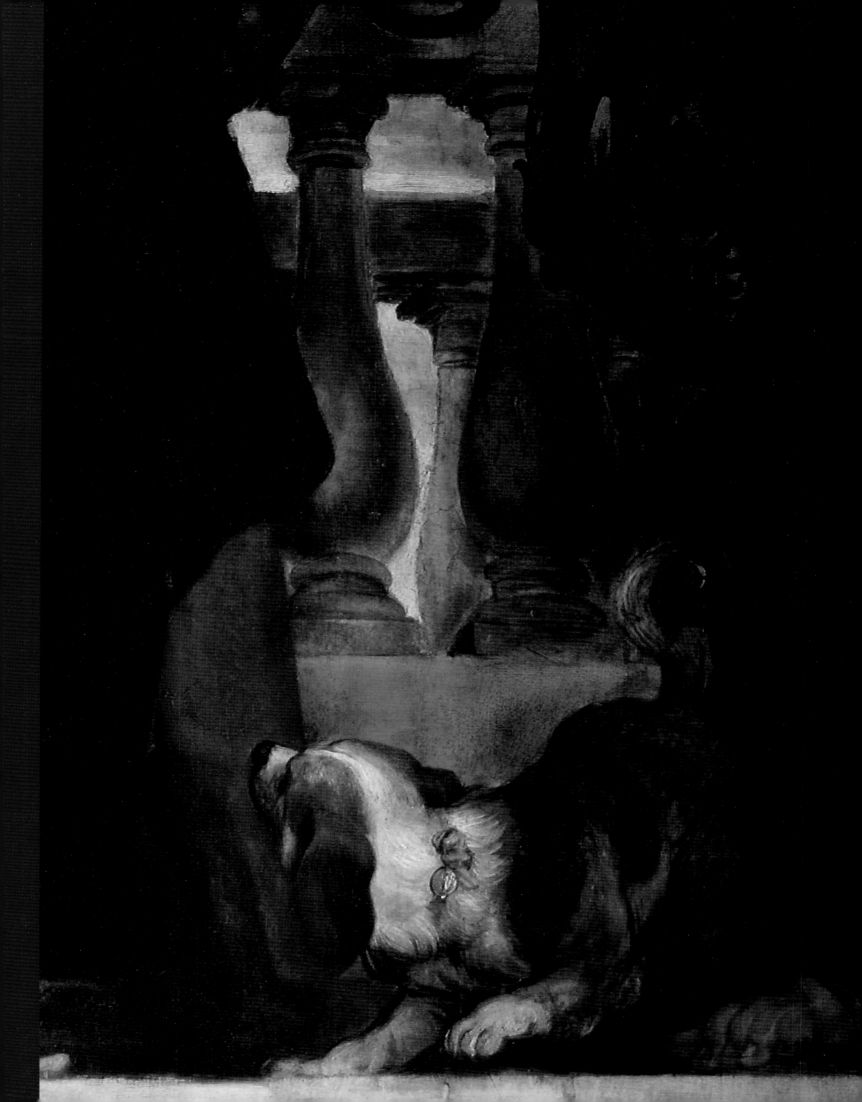

Peter Paul Rubens (1577–1640),
*The Raising of the Cross*, 1609–10,
oil on wood, 460 x 340 and 460 x 150 cm (x2)

Rubens had only just returned from Italy
when he painted this triptych for the high
altar in the Church of St Walburga. The
three panels form a continuous whole:
Mary, John and a group of horrified
women and children look on from the
left at the scene unfolding in the centre;
the right wing contains a group of Roman
soldiers carrying out their orders, together
with the two thieves who are also to be
crucified. The painting is 6.4 metres wide
and 4.6 metres high – unprecedentedly
large in 1610. That meant the panel had
to be hung fairly high, while remaining
clearly visible. The altar was 25 steps
higher than the nave. The shutters were
kept closed on ordinary days and were only
opened on Sundays and feast days.

The backs of the shutters are decorated with three saints who spent time in Antwerp during their lives: Amandus (seventh century; founder of St Walburga's), Walburga (eighth century; she lived in the church as a hermit) and Eligius (patron saint of Antwerp's smiths).

The Church expected artists in Rubens's time to show greater accuracy when it came to depicting scenes from the Gospels. It had become customary, for instance, to picture Mary swooning by the cross, whereas the Gospel of John states that she stood by it. Once again, the change alters the emphasis from weakness and defeat to strength, courage and ultimate triumph.

This work, too, is fully in the spirit of the Counter-Reformation. The muscular Christ, for instance, is anything but a broken man: He raises His head towards heaven and God the Father, from where salvation will come. With God's help, He will conquer death.

Master of the Mosan Marble Madonnas, *Virgin and Child*,
first half fourteenth century, white marble, height 127 cm

**Hans van Mildert (1588–1638),** *Saints Peter and Paul,* c. 1629–33, limestone, height 216 and 225 cm

St Peter (left) and St Paul (right) are two giants from the beginning of Christianity. They hold their traditional attributes: Peter – Apostle and first head of the Church – has the key to heaven, while Christian convert Paul holds a book and the sword with which he was beheaded during the reign of Emperor Nero.

Huibrecht van den Eynde (1594–1661), *Gideon*,
and Artus Quellinus the Younger (1625–1700),
*Joshua*, white marble, height 180 cm

Gideon and Joshua are both figures from
the Bible who were seen as liberators of the
Israelites and as warriors for the faith. It was
in that capacity that they originally stood
on the altar of the Swordsmen's Guild.

Artus Quellinus the Younger (1625–1700), *Virgin of the Immaculate Conception or Mary Triumphant*, white and black marble, height 112 cm

This is one of the many figures of the Virgin Mary in the cathedral: she stands on a crescent moon, trampling the serpent of evil. The young Jesus helps her to rid the world of wickedness. This is an image of Mary Triumphant or the Virgin of the Immaculate Conception.

Marius Ambrosius Capello, seventh Bishop of Antwerp, monumental tomb by Artus Quellinus the Younger (after 1676) and memorial sculpture (1676) by Hendrik Frans Verbrugghen

Bishop Capello was a philanthropist and patron of the cathedral, whose death in 1676 was greeted with much sorrow in the city. In his will, Capello left all his possessions to the poor. He was given both a splendid monumental tomb in the cathedral and a memorial sculpture. ▸

The tomb, which was originally located in the choir, is the only one to have survived the French Revolution. The praying figure of the bishop rests on a pillow and looks upwards. The little angel shows Capello's coat of arms.

Ill:mo ac Rev:mo Dño
F. AMBROSIO CAPELLO
ord: Prædicatorum
VII ANTVERP. EPISCOPO
in vita et in morte
ARCHI·ELEEMOSYNARIO
(dixi satis)
ELEEMOSYNARII ex asse hæredes
Pio et grato animo P. P.
MDCLXXVI

Michiel van der Voort the Elder (1667–1737),
pulpit, 1713, oak

The famous Cistercian abbey at Hemiksem, near Antwerp, was partially destroyed towards the end of the eighteenth century. The abbey church was one of the lost buildings. Several important fittings ended up at the Church of Our Lady, including a series of confessionals dating from 1713 by Guillielmus Ignatius Kerrickx (1682–1745) and Michiel van der Voort the Elder (1667–1737). The latter also carved the abbey church's brilliant pulpit. The main body of the pulpit, in which the priest stood, is supported by figures personifying the four continents as known in 1713, symbolizing the global reach of the Catholic faith. Europe holds a sceptre to indicate its mastery over the world. Asia is dressed in oriental robes, Africa is a black woman in a turban, and the woman representing America wears a feathered headdress.

St Bernard of Clairvaux, who founded the Cistercian Order, wrote that nature has the ability to inspire worshippers, as it, too, bears witness to God's handiwork. This explains the iconography of the stairs leading to the body of the pulpit: trunks, branches and twigs of oak and beech trees, together with familiar birds and small animals, including a parrot, a turkey, a heron, an owl and several squirrels.

## The cathedral in numbers

There has been a shrine to the Virgin Mary at this spot for over 1,000 years.

The construction of the cathedral took 166 years.

With a surface area of 8,000 m² and a volume of 73,250 m³, this is the largest Gothic church in the Low Countries.

The total length of the interior is 118 m.

The total width of the interior is 67 m (transept) and 53.5 m (nave).

There are 7 aisles and 125 columns, each supporting a weight of 400 tonnes.

The height of the nave is 28 m and that of the crossing dome 43 m.

The *Assumption* (Cornelis Schut) measures 5.8 m in diameter.

The cathedral has 55 stained-glass windows.

The oldest ceiling paintings, around the bosses in the choir, were done more than 600 years ago (*c.* 1391).

There are 4 masterpieces by Rubens in the cathedral.

The monumental Schyven organ has 4 keyboards and a set of pedals, 90 registers and 5,770 pipes.

Our Lady's Tower is 123 m high, the South Tower 65 m and the crossing tower 56 m.

There are 615 steps leading to the top of Our Lady's Tower.

The carillon has 49 bells.

The oldest bells were founded in 1459: they are 'Maria' and the former alarm-bell 'Gabriel', which is now the base bell in the carillon.

The heaviest bell is 'Carolus' (1507), which weighs 6,434 kg. It measures 2.12 m in diameter and is 1.65 m high.

# Cathedral timeline

**1124**
Earliest reliable reference to the Chapel of Our Lady (no visible traces of which remain). Elevated to parish church status to replace St Michael's.

**c. 1132**
Work begins on construction of Romanesque precursor to the current church (fragment of wall in the crypt).

**1220**
The Duke of Brabant gives adjoining land to allow the church to expand ('for the use of the Church of the Blessed Mary and of the Chapter').

**1273–85**
Extension work (1275 'novum opus').

**14th century**
Number of chantries and associated altars increases.

**1352**
Construction begins of Gothic church (just the choir at first?) around the earlier building, which is demolished in stages.

**1355–c. 1380**
Work halted because of political strife between Brabant and Flanders.

**1384–85**
First reference to altars in the new structure.

**1387–1411**
Vaulting of new choir completed, stained-glass windows installed in choir.

**1391**
Donation of stained-glass windows by William of Berchem.

**1419**
Foundations laid for North Tower. Plan for church with five (?) bays; West Front with two towers and a crossing tower. Design by Peeter Appelmans.

**1434**
Fire damages the choir.

**c. 1450**
Plans for five-bay church turned into current seven-bay configuration.

**c. 1450**
First reference to altars belonging to militia companies and craft guilds (having previously belonged only to chantries and confraternities).

**c. 1475**
Work on South Tower stops to allow completion of the nave. Tower finished as far as belfry arches.

**1482–87**
Final remains of old church demolished.

**1518**
Large tower completed.

**1519**
The 'new works' commence with the aim of tripling the existing floor area.

**1521**
Charles V lays first stone of new church.

**1533**
'New works' halted. Fire inflicts immense damage. Repairs are completed rapidly, but expansion plans are temporarily set aside.

**1537**
Donation of two stained-glass windows (by Fugger brothers and Burgomaster Dassa and his wife Barbara Rockox); craft guilds install altars again.

**1559**
Foundation of Diocese of Antwerp: the church becomes a cathedral.

**Aug. 1566**
Iconoclasts attack church.

**Nov. 1576**
Spanish Fury. Cathedral spared.

**1578**
Calvinist regime. The church is 'purified'.

**1585**
Restoration of Catholic worship following Farnese's reconquest of the city.

**17th century**
Much new art: mainly painting at first with greater emphasis subsequently on sculpture.

**1609**
Twelve Years' Truce begins: cathedral repaired and finished.

**18th century**
Cultural tourism begins to develop.

**1786**
Joseph II abolishes confraternities; their art treasures are auctioned.

**1794**
French troops march into Antwerp. Key works of art taken to Paris.

**1795**
Region annexed by French republic: monastic property confiscated, guilds abolished.

**1797**
Parishes abolished. Plans to demolish the cathedral.

**1798**
Cathedral contents auctioned off.

**19th century**
Refurbishment that continues until 1914: classical at first and then neo-Gothic.

**1800**
Church reopens. Rubble cleared up and refurbishment begins. Some of the auctioned 'salvage materials' are repurchased.

**1801**
Diocese of Antwerp abolished; the church is no longer a cathedral.

**1815**
Return of many of the works of art taken to Paris in 1794.

**1844–1917**
Second phase of restoration: South Tower, West Front, transept, choir and porches. Numerous neo-Gothic additions (e.g. porch sculptures).

**1961**
Diocese of Antwerp refounded: the church becomes a cathedral again.

**1965**
New round of restoration that will take decades to complete.

**June 1973**
Final service before the cathedral closes to allow large-scale works to be carried out.

**20 May 1983**
King Baudouin reopens the restored nave of the cathedral.

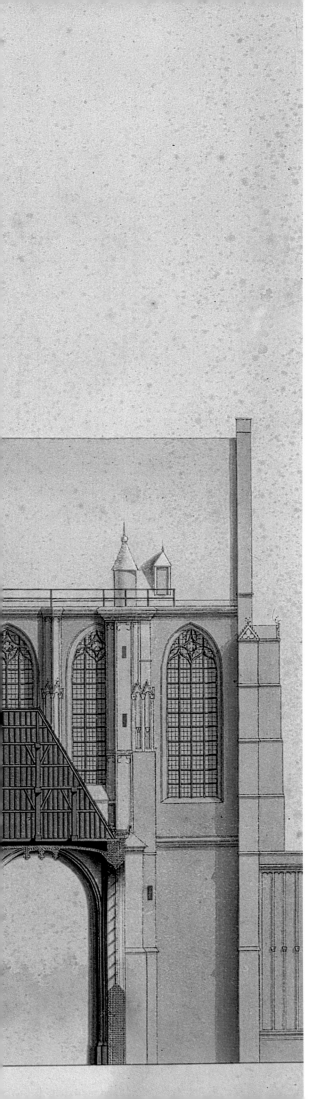

Drawing of the Cathedral by Jan Blom

Further reading

*A great deal has been written about the turbulent history of the cathedral and its art treasures. This book drew primarily on four recent publications:*

Willem Aerts (ed.), *The Cathedral of Our Lady in Antwerp*, Fonds Mercator, 1993. Comprehensive work including individual studies of the building, its artistic heritage, life in and around the church, restoration, music and archaeological research.

Jan van Damme, *The Cathedral of Our Lady in Antwerp*, Gemeentekrediet/Crédit Communal, 1994. Fascinating introduction to the cathedral, its architectural and general history and its contents.

Stefaan Grieten and Joke Bungeneers (eds), *De Onze-Lieve-Vrouwekathedraal van Antwerpen. Kunstpatrimonium van het ancien régime* (*Inventaris van het kunstpatrimonium van de provincie Antwerpen, 3*), Turnhout, Brepols, 1996. A complete scholarly inventory (in Dutch) up to the end of the eighteenth century.

Irene Smets, *The Cathedral of Our Lady in Antwerp*, Ghent, Ludion, 1999. Guide to the cathedral with descriptions of the key works of art together with text boxes on general themes.